Table of Contents

Amazing Winter Recipes That You Must Try

Unique Winter Recipes to Warm You Up

BY: Ida Smith

License Notes

Introduction

Winter is that time of the year when you need to put away your sexy tops and start wearing sweaters that will make you feel warm at all times. However, while you are busy whining about the cold weather, you should know that the winter season is cool and having some nice warmth. Meals will make your day. Winter comes with various nice dishes that will thrill you and right here in this cookbook are 30 unique recipes that will make you spend most of your time in the kitchen. However, before the end of winter, you would have succeeded in making all the meals in here.

Roasted potatoes

If you've ever had roasted potatoes, then you will agree that it is nice. You can have your crispy roasted potatoes any time of the day during winter.

Cooking Time: 70 minutes
Yield: 4
Ingredient List:

- 8 large potatoes
- 1/2 cup of oil
- 1 teaspoon of salt

Preparation:

Peel and boil your potatoes for about 10 minutes in boiling water. Drain the potatoes and half each one. Lay them on a chopping board as d use a fork to Ridge the face of each potatoes and add it to your roasting own.

Heat your oil in a roasting tray, then pour the hot oil on the surface of your potatoes, sprinkle salt in it and bake for about 50 minutes.

When it turns golden brown, remove and serve immediately.

Baked egg and asparagus

With a few and very simple ingredients, you have successfully prepared this meal, and when you bake it, it comes out really nice.

Cooking Time: 50 minutes
Yield: 4
Ingredient List:

- 2 tablespoons of oil
- 2 Cloves of well-minced garlic
- 1 well-sliced leek
- 1 teaspoon of salt
- 1 teaspoon of black pepper
- 8 big eggs
- 1/3 cup of heavy cream

- 1 tablespoon of Italian seasoning
- 2 cups of golden potatoes, diced
- 1 pound of asparagus, fresh and trimmed
- 1 can of goat cheese

Preparation:

Preheat your oven to about 350°. Heat your oil in your pan. Add leek and garlic to the pan and sauté for about 7 minutes. Season with half of the salt and half of your pepper, remove from heat and set aside.

Whisk your eggs in a large bowl, add your cream and seasoning, add your remaining salt and pepper then pour the mixture into a baking pan. Top with your potatoes, asparagus, and goat cheese put in the oven and bake for 40 minutes or until your potatoes are tender.

Remove from oven and serve hot.

Pasta casserole and sausage

Looking for a quick dinner? This pasta is your go-to meal and it is very satisfying.

Cooking Time: 50 minutes

Yield: 4

Ingredient List:

- 2 packs of pasta
- 2 tablespoons of oil
- 1 small-sized well-chopped onion
- 1 teaspoon of salt
- 1/3 tablespoon of black pepper
- 2 pounds of pork sausage
- 1 tablespoon of Italian seasoning
- 1 can of roasted diced tomatoes
- 1 cup of tomato sauce

- 1 cup of grated mozzarella
- 1/3 cup of grated parmesan

Preparation:

Preheat your oven to about 350°. Boil pasta in a pot of salted boiled water, drain and set aside. Heat oil in a pan, add onion and garlic. Season with your part of your salt and pepper and let it cook for another 10 minutes.

Add your sausage cook for 10 minutes, add your seasoning, add your roasted tomatoes, tomato sauce and the remaining pepper and salt and let it boil for another 10 minutes.

Remove from heat and add your pasta and mozzarella into the pan and mix properly. Transfer mixture to a baking dish, sprinkle your parmesan cheese on it and bake for 20 minutes, remove from oven and serve.

Spicy spinach soup

This soup is one of the easiest soups you can make, especially when the weather is very cold and you need to have a quick soup to keep you warm.

Cooking Time: 50 minutes
Yield: 6
Ingredient List:

- 3 tablespoons of oil
- 1 tablespoon of minced ginger
- 2 cloves of minced garlic
- 1 medium-sized yellow diced onion
- 1 teaspoon of salt
- 1/3 tablespoon of ground black pepper
- 2 teaspoons of curry powder

- 1 tablespoon of red pepper flakes
- 1 can of tomato sauce
- 1 can of drained chickpeas
- 1 cup of baby spinach

Preparation:

Heat your oil in a pan, add your garlic, onions and ginger and simmer for 10 minutes. Add your curry powder, salt, pepper, pepper flakes, tomato sauce, and chickpea and allow it to boil.

Add your spinach, and boil for another 20 minutes. Remove and serve.

Bacon and fish chowder soup

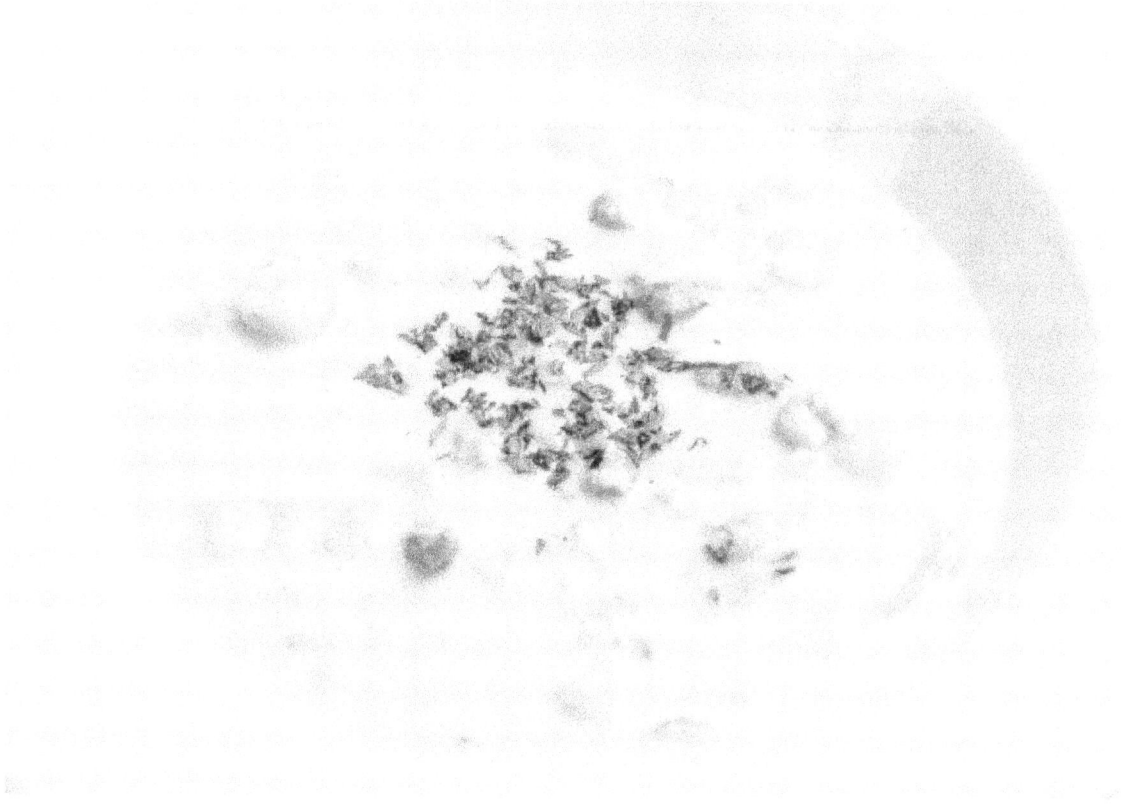

You can use any white fish of your choice to make this meal, and it is not only tasty but also nutritious.

Cooking Time: 40 minutes

Served: 4

Ingredient List:

- 4 pieces of unsmoked bacon
- 1 small chopped onion
- 3 tablespoons of flour
- 1 cup of fish stock
- 1/3 cup of white wine
- 1 lb. red potatoes, peeled and cut
- 1lb boneless and skinless white fish

- 1/2 cup of cream
- 2 tablespoons of fresh parsley, chopped
- 1 teaspoon of salt
- 1/2 teaspoon of white pepper.

Preparation:

Cut your bacon into cube sizes, add it to your pan with oil and simmer until it becomes brown and the fat turns to liquid. Add your onions and fry for another 5 minutes. Add your flour and stir it, then add your stock and mix properly.

Add the wine and potatoes and boil for further 15 minutes. Then heat your cream in a small pan and add it to the soup.

Add your fish and let it boil, add your salt and pepper to taste, sprinkle your parsley on it and serve hot.

Chicken, corn, and cheese casserole

This is the recipe that you will love to have during the winter season. It is not only spicy, but also very delicious and the taste of corn muffins in it makes it more amazing.

Cooking Time: 40 minutes
Yield: 6
Ingredient List:

- 1 cup of cheddar cheese, shredded and divided
- 1/2 can of milk
- 4 big eggs, whisked
- 1/2 tablespoon of ground cumin
- 1 can of corn, creamed
- 6 ounce of corn muffin mixture
- 2 big green chilies, chopped

- 1 cup of enchilada sauce, red preferable
- 3 cups of shredded cooked chicken
- 1/2 cup of monetary jack cheese, shredded
- 2 tablespoons of chopped cilantro

Preparation:

Preheat your oven to about 380°. Mix half of your cheddar cheese, milk, eggs, cumin, corn muffin, creamed corn, and green chilies in a bowl, combine properly and transfer mixture to a casserole dish and bake for about 20 minutes.

Put holes on the top with a fork and pour your enchilada sauce on it. Place your shredded chicken on it, add your monetary cheese and cheddar cheese to it and return it back to the oven for another 15 minutes.

When it bubbles, remove from oven, garnish with your cilantro and serve hot.

Baked chicken and rice

Maybe you've never have baked rice and chicken before and this recipe may sound weird, but a trial will convince you of how tasty this meal is.

Cooking Time: 70 minutes
Yield: 4
Ingredient List:

- 1 cup of brown rice
- 2 medium-sized diced carrot
- 1/3 cup of broccoli
- 1/2 cup of frozen peas
- 1 tablespoon of salt
- 1/3 tablespoon of ground black pepper
- 3 cups of chicken broth

- 2 tablespoons of butter
- 2 chicken breasts, skinless and boneless
- 1/4 tablespoon of dry thyme

Preparation:

Preheat your oven to about 360°. Mix your rice, carrot, broccoli, and peas in a bowl and mix properly. Pour the mixture into a casserole dish, season with a little salt and pepper. Pour your broth over the rice and veggies and top your butter.

Add your chicken breast to the pan, add thyme and your remaining salt and pepper cover the pan with a foil and bake for about 55 minutes. Remove from oven and serve hot.

Baked tuna and noodles

Your winter cannot be completed without having this meal. It is understandable that the weather is cold and going out to eat is difficult. So, you can have this quickly from your home.

Cooking Time: 30 minutes

Yield: 6

Ingredient List:

- 1 pack of dried egg noodles
- 1/2 cup of butter
- 1/3 cup of flour
- 1/3 tablespoon of garlic powder
- 1/2 tablespoon of salt
- 1/2 teaspoon of ground pepper
- 3 cups of milk

- 2 tablespoons of parmesan cheese
- 1 can of frozen peas
- 2 cans of drained and flaked tuna
- 2 tablespoons of breadcrumbs
- 1 tablespoon of thyme leaves

Preparation:

Heat up your oven to about 360°. Boil water in a large pot and add salt to it. When the water boils, add your noodles and cook for 5 minutes, drain and set aside. Mix part of your butter and flour in a bowl, add your garlic, salt, and pepper, put mixture in a pot and heat up a little. Gradually add your milk and stir properly until your sauce thickens.

Add your parmesan cheese into the mixture and remove the pot from heat. Add your noodles, tuna, and peas in the pot and mix well. Mix your breadcrumbs and remaining butter and thyme in another bowl, pour your mixture into a casserole and add your breadcrumb mixture on it, bake for 20 minutes or until it becomes brown, remove from oven and serve hot.

Frozen peas and ham casserole

This dish can be served any time of the year, but it is perfect for that snowy day that you need to stay warm all day.

Cooking Time: 35 minutes
Yield: 6
Ingredient List:

- 16 ounces of pasta
- 1/2 cup of oil
- 3 cloves of minced garlic
- 1 pack of frozen peas
- 1/3 pound of diced ham
- 1 teaspoon of salt
- 1/3 tablespoon of fresh ground pepper

- 1 cup of heavy cream
- 1 cup of chicken broth
- 1 tablespoon of grated parmesan cheese
- 2 tablespoons of breadcrumbs

Preparation:
Preheat your oven to 400°. Boil your pasta in salted water until it is tender, drain and return pasta to the pot. Add a little oil and toss so it doesn't get sticky. Heat your remaining oil in another pan, add your garlic and simmer for 5 minutes. Add your peas and ham, cook until your peas become hot, and then season with salt and pepper.

Then add your cream, stock, and cook until it thickens. Pour your sauce into the pasta, add your parmesan, mix properly and transfer to your casserole dish.

Top with your breadcrumbs and bake for 20 minutes and serve hot.

Chicken in sour cream

This is a very simple meal to prepare and it is very nourishing and you can serve it with your rice or pasta.

Cooking Time:25 minutes
Yield: 4
Ingredient List:

- 1/2 cup of butter
- 2 tablespoons of paprika
- 1 medium-sized well chopped onion
- 3 chicken breasts, cut in cubes
- 1 tablespoon of salt
- 1 teaspoon of ground black pepper
- 2 cups of chicken broth
- 1 cup of water

- 1 tablespoon of cornstarch
- 1/2 cup of sour cream

Preparation:

Heat your pan and add your butter, when it melts, add your paprika to the pan, stir and add onion then let it cook for about 10 minutes. Add your chicken, salt, and pepper, stir often and let it cook for like 5 minutes.

Add your chicken broth gradually and allow the mixture to boil, and the chicken is well cooked. Mix your water and cornstarch in a small bowl until it is smooth then add it to the sauce and cook for another 5 minutes or until it becomes thick.

Add your sour cream, remove from heat and serve while hot.

Spicy sausage stew

This is a special meal that you can prepare with the regular ingredients you have at home.

Cooking Time: 30 minutes

Yield: 4

Ingredient List:

- 3 tablespoons of oil
- 1 clove of minced garlic
- 1 medium-sized, diced onion
- 1/3 tablespoon of salt
- 1/2 teaspoon of ground black pepper
- 1/2 tablespoon of paprika
- 1/3 tablespoon of dried oregano
- 2 bells of chopped red peppers

- 1 bell of chopped yellow pepper
- 4 Italian sausages
- 1 teaspoon of tomato puree
- 1/2 cup of red wine
- 1 can of chopped tomato

Preparation:

Heat your oil in a pan. Add your onions and garlic and simmer for about 5 minutes, add your salt, pepper, oregano, and paprika, then add your bell peppers and cook for another 5 minutes. Add your sausage to the pan, coon for another 10 minutes.

Add your tomato puree, and mix your red wine and cook. Add your chopped tomato and allow your area to boil. Once it boils you serve hot.

Hot shrimp sauce

What the winter season needs is something hot and spicy, and here is one simple and spicy meal to prepare.

Cooking Time: 30 minutes
Yield: 4
Ingredient List:

- 1/2 cup of oil
- 2 medium-sized well chopped yellow onions
- 4 cloves of minced garlic
- 2 big carrot, chopped
- 1 big potato, cubed
- 1 teaspoon of cayenne pepper
- 1/3 tablespoon of ground cumin

- 1/2 teaspoon of salt
- 1/3 teaspoon of pepper
- 1 bay leaf
- 2 pounds of large raw shrimp, peeled and deveined
- 1/3 cup of tomato paste
- 1 cup of white wine
- 1/2 cup of water
- 1/3 cup of lemon juice
- 2 big green onions, minced

Preparation:

Heat your oil in a pan, add onions and garlic and let it sauté for 3 minutes. Add your carrot and potato and let it cook for another 5 minutes. Add cayenne pepper and part of your cumin into the pan, add salt, pepper and your bay leaf into the pan and cook for about 10 minutes.

Season your shrimp with your leftover cayenne pepper and cumin, add your tomato paste and let it cook for a few minutes, then add in your white wine, water, and lime juice and let it boil for another 5 minutes.

Add your shrimp and cook for another 5 minutes, and serve hot, while you garnish it with your green onions.

Baked chard and sausage

When you try this recipe, you will learn to appreciate how simple it is to prepare and how tasty it can be.

Cooking Time: 30 minutes

Yield: 4

Ingredient List:

- 10 ounces of pasta
- 1/2 cup of oil
- 4 cloves of minced garlic
- 1 medium sized onion, diced
- 1 cup of swiss chard
- 1 pound of sausage
- 1/2 tablespoon of red pepper flakes
- 1/2 teaspoon of dried basil

- 1 teaspoon of salt
- 1/3 tablespoon of ground black pepper
- 1/3 cup of chopped parmesan

Preparation:

Heat your oven to 400°. Cook your pasta in boiling and salt water, when soft drain and return the last to the pot. Add a little oil and set aside. In another pan, add your remaining oil, when hot, add your garlic and onion and cook for about 10 minutes.

Then add your Swiss chard cook for another 2 minutes, add your sausage, and then season with pepper flakes, basil, salt, and pepper and cook for about 7 minutes. Add your pasta to the pan, mix everything together, and bake for about 10 minutes.

Remove from oven, sprinkle your parmesan cheese on it, and serve.

Baked noodles and beef

This meal is not only delicious and nutritious but also fun to prepare. Your family will love it!

Cooking Time: 60 minutes
Yield: 5
Ingredient List:

- 2 tablespoons of oil
- 10 oz beef, ground
- 1/2 tablespoon of salt
- 1/2 teaspoon of ground black pepper
- 1 cup of finely diced carrot
- 1 pack of pasta
- 4 big eggs
- 2 cups of ricotta cheese

- 1 cup of flour
- 2 cups of cheddar cheese

Preparation:

Preheat your oven to about 360°. Heat oil in a pan, add your beef, a little salt, and a little pepper and let it cook for about 5 minutes. Add your carrot and simmer for another 5 minutes, remove from pan and set aside.

Cook your pasta in boiling salted water, drain and set aside also. Mix your eggs, ricotta cheese, flour, and your remaining pepper and salt in a goal and transfer mixture to a baking dish, sprinkle your cheddar cheese on it and allow to bake for another 40 minutes.

Remove from oven, set aside to cool a little and serve.

Baked broccoli and egg

You need to try this recipe because mixing broccoli and eggs gives you the perfect flavor and when baked, you will enjoy it even more.

Cooking Time: 40 minutes
Yield: 5
Ingredient List:

- 2 tablespoons of butter
- 1 clove of minced garlic
- 1 large onion, diced
- 1 red bell pepper, chopped
- 1/3 cup of broccoli flower
- 1/2 tablespoon of salt
- 1 teaspoon of pepper

– 8 big eggs
– 1/3 cup of half and half

Preparation:
Heat your oven to about 360°. Heat butter in a pan, add garlic and onion and simmer for 5 minutes. Add your red bell pepper and broccoli and cook for another 5 minutes. Season with half of your salt and half of the pepper then pour the mixture into a baking pan.

Whisk your eggs in a bowl, ass your half and half and season with your remaining salt and pepper. Pour your eggs in the baking dish and bake for about 25 minutes.

Remove and serve hot.

Baked potato and ground beef

This is a mixture that you will enjoy from under your blankets. Serving it hot is perfect for this winter.

Cooking Time: 70 minutes

Yield: 4

Ingredient List:

- 2 tablespoons of oil
- 1 pound of beef, ground
- 1 teaspoon of salt
- 1/2 tablespoon of ground black pepper
- 1 small sized finely diced onion
- 2 cloves of minced garlic
- 1 cup of sour cream
- 8oz of cream cheese
- 2 cups of cheddar cheese, shredded

- 2 pounds of potatoes, peeled and sliced
- 3 well-minced scallions

Preparation:

Preheat your oven to about 360°. Heat oil in a large pan, add your beef, a little salt, and a little pepper, and cook for another 5 minutes. Add your onion and garlic and let it cook for another 10 minutes.

Mix your sour cream, cheddar cheese, cream cheese, salt, and pepper in a bowl and mix properly. Then add the potatoes and your beef mixture, mix properly and transfer to a baking dish and bake for about 50 minutes.

Garnish it with your scallions and serve hot.

Spicy red lentil soup

Soups are great for the cold and combining them with red lentils makes it more amazing. Using this recipe, we added sweet potatoes that makes it very rich and appetizing.

Cooking Time: 35 minutes

Yield: 4

Ingredient List:

- 3 tablespoons of oil
- 3 cloves of minced garlic
- 1 medium-sized yellow chopped onion
- 2 medium-sized peeled and diced potatoes
- 1 large peeled and diced carrot
- 1 teaspoon of salt
- 1/2 teaspoon of red pepper flakes

- 1 can of chopped tomatoes, drained
- 1/2 tablespoon of paprika
- 1/3 tablespoon of curry powder
- 1 cup of red lentil
- 3 cups of vegetable broth
- 2 cups of water
- 1 teaspoon of fresh ground black pepper
- 1 tablespoon of lemon juice

Preparation:
Put oil in a large pot and heat over medium heat. Add garlic and onions and cook for 5 minutes. Season with salt and pepper flakes. Add your chopped tomatoes, paprika, and curry powder and stir.

Add your red lentils, both, and water, allow it to boil until your veggies and lentils are soft.

Serve with your black pepper and lemon juice got.

White bean sauce

After preparing this meal, it will be the best meal you've had in a long while, and it will be great to have it with your family.

Cooking Time: 40 minutes
Yield: 4
Ingredient List:

- 2 tablespoons of oil
- 3 cloves of minced garlic
- 1 large diced yellow onion
- 1 teaspoon of salt
- 1/3 tablespoon of black pepper
- 5 pieces of Italian sausage
- 1 tablespoon of herbs

- 1/2 tablespoon of red pepper flakes
- 1 can of white beans
- 1 tablespoon of Italian seasoning
- 1 can of roasted diced tomatoes
- 1 cup of diced tomato
- 1 cup of chicken broth
- 1 cup of kale, chopped
- 2 tablespoons of minced parsley

Preparation:

Heat oil in a pan, add your garlic and onion. Season with your part of your salt and pepper and let it cook for another 10 minutes.

Add your sausage cook for 10 minutes, add your herb seasoning and red pepper flakes, add your roasted tomatoes, white beans, chicken broth, kale and your remaining salt and let it boil for another 10 minutes. Once your sauce is ready, serve hot. And garnish with your parsley.

Baked cheese and pasta

This dish is an amazing meal and for most people, it has become their favorite meal.

Cooking Time: 35 minutes
Yield: 8
Ingredient List:

- 1 pack of pasta
- 1/2 cup of flour
- 1/2 cup of butter
- 4 cups of milk
- 1 tablespoon of dry mustard
- 1/2 teaspoon of paprika
- 1 teaspoon of nutmeg, ground
- 1/2 teaspoon of salt

- 3 cups of grated cheddar cheese
- 2 cups of Romano cheese

Preparation:

Preheat your oven to about 360°. Boil your pasta in a pot of boiling salt water, when soft, remove, drain, and set aside. Add butter in a large pan and heat until it melts, add your flour and cook for about 5 minutes. Add your milk gradually, stirring often and cook until it becomes thick.

Add your dry mustard, nutmeg, salt, paprika, Romano cheese, and part of your cheddar cheese. Mix properly until your cheese dissolves and your sauce smooth and, remove from heat.

Add your pasta into the sauce, coat properly, sprinkle your remaining cheese on it, pour into a baking dish and bake for about 25 minutes or your cheese melts. Remove from oven and serve hot.

Baked bacon and potato

Bacon and potato are a perfect combination that can be served in between meals and a perfect way to treat your family during the winter.

Cooking Time: 65 minutes
Yield: 5
Ingredient List:

- 2 tablespoons of oil
- 1 pound of sliced bacon, diced
- 2 medium-sized yellow onions, chopped
- 3 cloves of minced garlic
- 1 teaspoon of kosher salt,
- 1 teaspoon of ground black pepper
- 2 pounds of diced red potatoes

– 2 cups of cheese, grated and divided

Preparation:

Preheat the oven to about 360°. Heat your oil in a pan, add your onions, bacon, and garlic, then season with a little salt, a little pepper, and cook for another 10 minutes. Mix your potatoes, cheese, and bacon mixture in a bowl, add your remaining salt and pepper, transfer into a baking dish, cover with foil and bake for about 50 minutes.

Remove and serve hot.

Baked mushroom and green beans

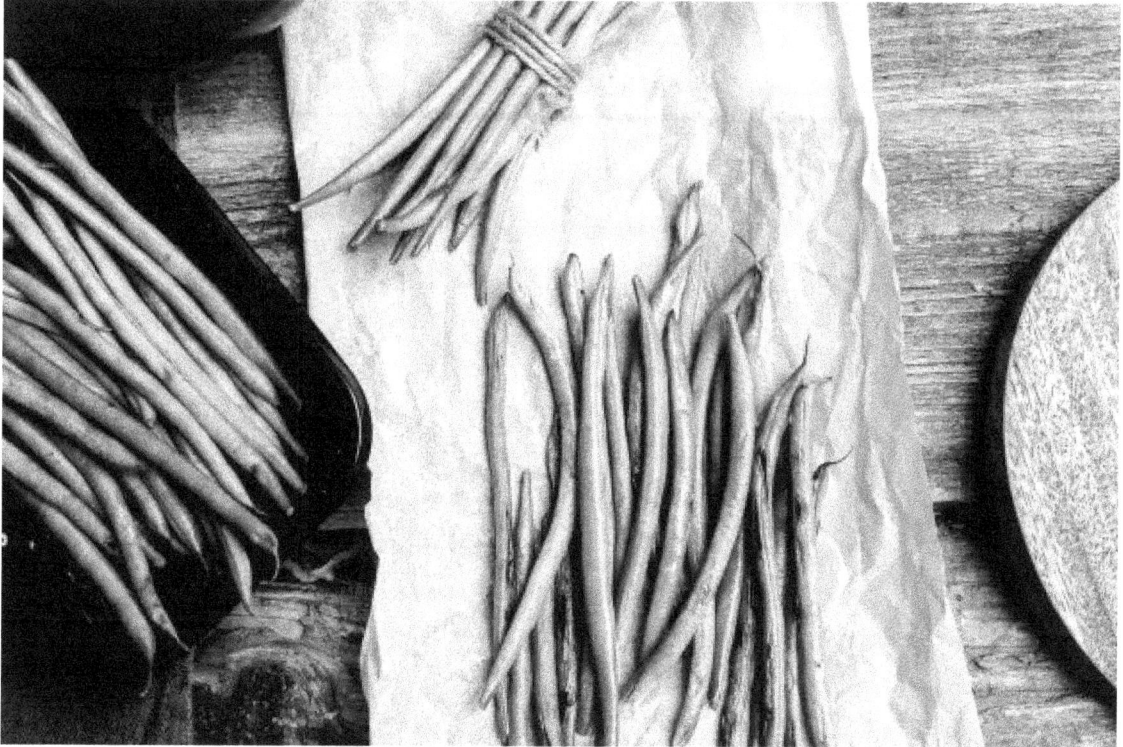

When you are ready to cozy up with your family and watch that blockbuster movie while having dinner, then this is the perfect dinner to make.

Cooking Time: 35 minutes
Yield: 6
Ingredient List:

- 2 cups of chicken broth
- 4 cups of trimmed green beans
- 2 tablespoons of butter
- 1 cup of mushrooms, sliced
- 1 can of cream mushroom soup
- 1/2 cup of milk
- 1 teaspoon of Worcestershire sauce
- 1 cup of cheddar cheese, shredded

– 1 cup of French-fried onions

Preparation:

Heat up your oven to about 300°. Mix your broth and green beans in a pan and allow to boil, when the green beans are soft, remove and drain. Add butter in the pan, add your mushroom and simmer for 5 minutes then remove your mushrooms and add to your green beans.

Add your mushroom soup, milk, Worcestershire sauce, cheese, French fried, into the green beans, and transfer to a baking dish. Bake for about 30 minutes, and when it begins to bubble, remove and serve hot.

Potatoes and cheese

While the weather is cold, there's nothing as good as having a good and warm dinner. And this dish is perfect for you.

Cooking Time: 55 minutes
Yield: 4
Ingredient List:

- 1/2 cup of butter
- 1/2 cup of flour
- 3 cups of milk
- 1 tablespoon of salt
- ½ teaspoon of ground black pepper
- 1 teaspoon of paprika
- 1 cup of grated white cheddar cheese, grated

- 1 cup of grated cheese, grated
- 5 large potatoes, sliced.
- 2 tablespoons of minced parsley

Preparation:

Preheat the oven to about 375°. In a pan, heat the butter, once your butter has melted, add your flour and whisk slowly and continuously for about 2 to 3minutes. Gradually add your milk and whisk to remove all of the lumps and continue to cook for another 5 minutes until the sauce thickens.

Remove the pan from heat and season with your salt, paprika, and pepper, add part of your cheddar cheese and part of your gruyere cheese. Add part of your potatoes to a baking pan, add your cheese sauce sprinkle your remaining cheese on it and bake until your potatoes are tender.

Remove from oven, garnish with your parsley and serve.

Baked parsnips

Parsnips should be used often because they are an amazing ingredient. Therefore, this recipe is one that you must try because it's going to be delicious.

Cooking Time: 50 minutes
Yield: 4
Ingredient List:

- 1 tablespoon of butter
- 2 tablespoons of flour
- 1 cup of milk
- 1 cup of grated Parmesan cheese
- 1 tablespoon of chopped fresh thyme
- 1 teaspoon of salt
- 1/2 teaspoon of ground black pepper

- 4 peeled and chopped parsnips
- 1/3 cup of grated gruyere cheese

Preparation:

Preheat your oven to 360°. Heat your pan and add your butter and flour, mix properly. Pour your milk gradually into the mixture and stud for about 3 minutes. Remove pan from heat and add half of your parmesan cheese, thyme, salt and pepper.

Pour half of your mixture into a baking dish, spread your parsnip on it, and pour your remaining mixture on it. Sprinkle with your gruyere cheese and bake for about 40 minutes.

Once the top is brown, remove from given and serve hot.

Baked vegetables

This meal can be paired with a very good roasted chicken and it is very easy to prepare. You can make this on a cold morning for the family.

Cooking Time: 60 minutes
Yield: 4
Ingredient List:

- 1/2 cup of oil
- 4 small parsnips
- 6 big Carrot
- 1 small-sized sliced swede
- 1 bell of red pepper
- 2 teaspoons of fresh rosemary
- 1 teaspoon of salt

Preparation:

Preheat your oven to about 200°. Add part of your oil into a pan, heat pan until your oil sizzles. Add your parsnip, carrot, swede, mix with the oil and season with your pepper, rosemary, and salt.

Add your remaining oil and transfer mixture to a baking pan, bake for about 45 minutes or until your veggies turn brown and serve.

Baked Zucchini and cheese

There's nothing as good as having a fresh zucchini in your home during the cold and snowy days, and guess what? Cooking it at your comfort home tastes better than what you have in restaurants.

Cooking Time: 40 minutes
Yield: 5
Ingredient List:

- 2 tablespoons of oil
- 4 cloves of well-minced garlic
- 5 medium-sized sliced zucchinis
- 1 teaspoon of salt
- 1/2 teaspoon of black pepper
- 2 cups of evaporated milk
- 1 cup of cheddar cheese, grated

– 3 medium-sized green onions, diced

Preparation:

Preheat your oven to 360°. Heat your oil in a pan, add your garlic and zucchini and simmer for about 7 minutes or until your zucchini is tender. Season it with a little salt and pepper.

Remove from heat and pour mixture into a casserole dish. Heat the own again and pour your milk in to it and allow it to boil and season with your remaining salt. Add part of your cheddar cheese into the milk, stir until it is smooth then pour the mixture over your zucchini, sprinkle with your remaining cheese and bake for about 30 minutes.

Remove from oven, serve in a serving bowl, sprinkle your green onions on it and serve sizzling.

Spicy pumpkin soup

Easy to make spicy pumpkin soup is perfect for that snowy day. When you need to stay warm and cozy, this soup is perfect.

Cooking Time: 50 minutes
Yield: 6
Ingredient List:

- 1 big peeled and chopped pumpkin
- 1 medium-sized onion diced
- 2 cups of vegetable broth
- 2 cups of water
- 1/2 cup of full cream
- 1 teaspoon of ground black pepper
- 1/2 teaspoon of salt

Preparation:

Put your pumpkin, onion, vegetable broth, and water in a pan and let it boil for about 20 minutes or until your pumpkin is soft. Then put it in a food processor and blend until it becomes smooth.

Return to pan, add your salt and pepper, simmer for 15 minutes, add your cream, and serve.

Baked macaroni and broccoli

Here is another baked pasta that will please you and your family. It does magic to your mouth and it is perfect for the cool winter morning.

Cooking Time: 45 minutes
Yield: 6
Ingredient List:

- 3 cups of macaroni
- 4 cups of broccoli
- 1/3 cup of butter
- 1/3 cup of flour
- 1/2 teaspoon of garlic powder
- 1/3 teaspoon of onion powder
- 1/2 teaspoon of salt

- 1/2 teaspoon of ground pepper
- 2 cups of cream
- 2 cups of grated cheddar cheese
- 1/2 cup of breadcrumbs

Preparation:

Heat up your oven to about 360°. Boil your macaroni bin a pot of salt water for about 5 minutes. Add your broccoli and cook for extra 5 minutes, then drain and set aside. Add butter in a pan and once it melts add our flour, garlic, onion, salt, and pepper and let it simmer for 5 minutes.

Add your cream, stir well and let it boil for another 5 minutes. Add your cheese, pasta and broccoli, coat properly and transfer to a casserole dish. Sprinkle your remaining cheese on it and bake for about 30 minutes.

Remove from oven and serve hot.

Baked cheese and tomatoes

If you try this meal once, it might turn out to be your favorite winter meal. It's a simple Mexican meal and it's very tasty.

Cooking Time: 30 minutes
Yield: 8
Ingredient List:

- 8 corn tortillas, white
- 1 cup of thinly shredded cabbage
- 2 diced sweet tomatoes
- 4 cups of cheddar cheese
- 1 can of enchilada sauce
- 1/3 cup of goat cheese, crumbled
- 2 tablespoons of sour cream

Preparation:

Preheat your oven to about 180°. Heat your tortillas in a pan for 1 minute. Place your enchilada sauce in a dish. Fill each tortilla with cheese, roll it securely and place the seam side down in a pan. Pour your remaining sauce on it, sprinkle with your remaining cheese and bake for about 30 minutes then remove from oven.

Add your cabbage, tomatoes, goat cheese, and sour cream and serve hot.

Spicy skink soup

You can move out of your usual specialty and try this Scottish soup of fish. It is tasty and satisfying.

Cooking Time: 70 minutes
Yield: 5
Ingredient List:

- 1 lb. smoked haddock
- 1 bay leaf
- 2 tablespoons of butter
- 1 small-sized well diced onion
- 1 cup of whole milk
- 2 medium-sized peeled and chopped potatoes
- 1/2 cup of chopped chives
- 1 teaspoon of salt

– 1/2 tablespoon of ground black pepper

Preparation:

Put your fish in a pan, add water and bay lead and boil until your dish is cooked then transfer to a bowl and set aside to cool. Melt your butter in another pan and add your onions, cover and simmer for about 10 minutes. Season with your pepper and salt.

Add your potato into the butter, add your bacon juice and bay leaf and cook until your potato is soft. Remove bone and skin from your haddock and shred it, then remove your potato and bay leaf from pan and set aside.

Add your milk and haddock in a pan, stir until it becomes smooth,

Serve with your potato, and sprinkle chives on it.

Spicy leek and potato soup

Want to make something spicy for dinner? You can never go wrong with this delicious and spicy soup.

Cooking Time: 45 minutes
Yield: 4
Ingredient List:

- 1 small-sized onion
- 2 pieces of leeks
- 3 big potatoes
- 1/3 cup of butter
- 4 cups of chicken broth
- 1 teaspoon of salt
- 1 teaspoon of black ground pepper

Preparation:

Wash your leeks and slice, removing the ends. Dice your onions and set aside. Peel and also dice your potatoes.

In a large pan, heat part of your butter, add onions and leeks and site until it becomes transparent. Add your potatoes and let it simmer for another 2 minutes. Add your broth, salt and pepper and cook for about 30 minutes while stirring often.

Remove from heat, add your remaining butter, stir and serve hot.

Conclusion

Winter season is a time when one wants to relax and have good meals from the comfort of their home. No one wants to walk about in the cold and snowy days in search of the restaurant which is why we have compiled 30 amazing and unique winter season meals that will keep you and your family warm. Cheers!

Don't miss out!

Visit the website below and you can sign up to receive emails whenever Ida Smith publishes a new book. There's no charge and no obligation.

https://books2read.com/r/B-A-LRXL-EELLB

BOOKS 2 READ

Connecting independent readers to independent writers.

Did you love *Amazing Winter Recipes That You Must Try: Unique Winter Recipes To Warm You Up*? Then you should read *Recipes with Nuts and Seeds: Tasty nuts and seeds food ideas to step up your food game*[1] by Ida Smith!

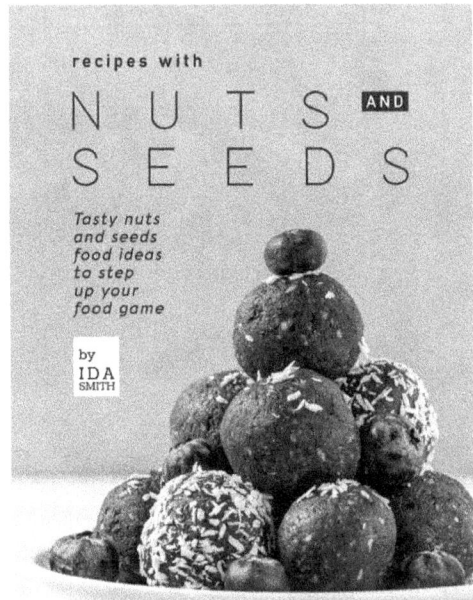

Nuts and seeds seem to form part of our regular menu and it is almost impossible to have a day roll past without a plate of seeds or nuts if you aren't a vegetarian. With this reality, finding easy and fun seeds and nuts recipes is finally yours and with a glance, you can make mealtime a fun time with 30 amazing nuts and seeds recipes. So, ditch the regular style you have been making for many years and explore that there's so much to make this year with nuts and seeds.

---

1. https://books2read.com/u/3n8VAx

2. https://books2read.com/u/3n8VAx

www.ingramcontent.com/pod-product-compliance
Lightning Source LLC
Chambersburg PA
CBHW081300040426
42452CB00014B/2581

* 9 7 8 1 3 9 3 1 7 3 4 0 3 *